My Pet

My Turtle

By Cate Foley

Welcome
Books

Children's Press
A Division of Grolier Publishing
New York / London / Hong Kong / Sydney
Danbury, Connecticut

Photo Credits: Cover, pp. 5, 21 by Maura Boruchow; p. 7 © Kennan Ward/Corbis; p. 9 © Wolfgang Kaehler/Corbis; p. 11 © Dave G. Houser/Corbis; p. 13 © Robert Pickett/Corbis; p. 15 © Kennan Ward/Corbis; p. 17 © Stephen Frink/Corbis; p. 19 © Kennan Ward/Corbis
Contributing Editor: Jeri Cipriano
Book Design: Nelson Sa

Visit Children's Press on the Internet at:
http://publishing.grolier.com

Library of Congress Cataloging-in-Publication Data

Foley, Cate.
   My turtle / by Cate Foley.
     p. cm.—(My pet)
   Includes bibliographical references and index.
   ISBN 0-516-23188-X (lib. bdg.)—ISBN 0-516-23291-6 (pbk.)
   1. Turtles as pets—Juvenile literature. [1. Turtles. 2. Pets.] I. Title. II. My pet (Children's Press)

 SF459. T8 F66 2000
 639.3′92—dc21   00-060099

Contents

A turtle would be a
good pet.

A turtle has a hard shell.

Its shell can be very beautiful.

5

How can I find a turtle
that is right for me?

6

Would a sea turtle make a good pet?

It lives in the ocean and can swim very fast.

9

It lays its eggs on the beach.

I think this turtle is best in the sea.

11

Would a leatherback turtle make a good pet?

It needs a lot of space because it grows very big.

A leatherback turtle can weigh one thousand pounds!

Maybe this turtle is not right for me.

Would a **tortoise** make a good pet?

A tortoise is a turtle that lives only on land.

This tortoise lives in the hot **desert**.

I live in the cool mountains.

Maybe this turtle is not right for me.

19

I looked and I looked.

I thought and I thought.

I think this turtle is just right for me!

New Words

desert (**dez**-ert) a dry, sandy place without water or trees

tortoise (**tor**-tuhs) a turtle that lives only on land

To Find Out More

Books

My Little Book of Painted Turtles
by Hope Irvin Marston
Creative Publishing International

Turtle Time
by Sandal Stoddard
Houghton Mifflin Company

Web Sites

Gulf of Maine Aquarium: All About Turtles

http://octopus.gma.org/turtles

This is an official site of the Gulf of Maine Aquarium. Here you can learn more about turtles, including information about how they live, how each body part helps them, and how they defend themselves.

Turtlehaven's Home Page

http://www.turtlehaven.com

This site provides information about a few different species of turtles. It also provides details about what they eat and where they live.

23

Index

About the Author
Cate Foley writes and edits books for children. She lives in New Jersey with her husband and son.

Reading Consultants
Kris Flynn, Coordinator, Small School District Literacy, The San Diego County Office of Education

Shelly Forys, Certified Reading Recovery Specialist, W.J. Zahnow Elementary School, Waterloo, IL

Peggy McNamara, Professor, Bank Street College of Education, Reading and Literacy Program